Amazing life cycles
REPTILES
and AMPHIBIANS
by Brian Williams

ticktock

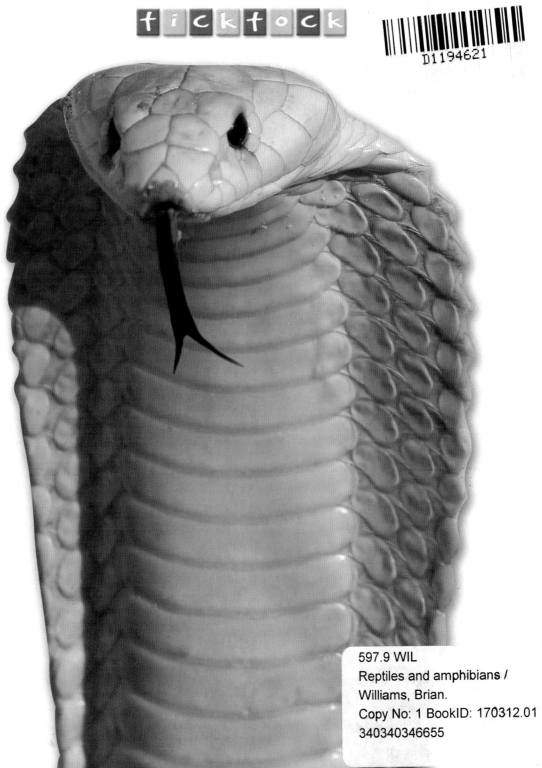

Copyright © ticktock Entertainment Ltd 2007

First published in Great Britain in 2007 by ticktock Media Ltd,
2 Orchard Business Centre, North Farm Road, Tunbridge Wells, Kent, TN2 3XF

ticktock project editor: Ruth Owen
ticktock project designer: Sara Greasley
With thanks to: Trudi Webb, Sally Morgan and Elizabeth Wiggans

ISBN 978-1-84696-071-0 pbk

Printed in China

Picture credits (t=top; b=bottom; c=centre; l=left; r=right):
FLPA: 4b, 5t, 6b, 7b, 11b, 17t, 18b, 25t, 25b, 26–27 all. Nature Picture Library: 16b, 19t, 23t, 29t. NHPA: 28–29 main, 31t. Shutterstock: OFC, 1, 2, 3, 4c, 6t, 8tl, 8b, 9, 10, 12tl, 13c, 13b, 14–15 all, 20 all,22tl, 22–23, 24tl, 24–25b, 30tl, 31b, OBC. Superstock: 5b, 8c, 11t, 13t, 16tl, 17b,18tl, 19b, 21t, 21b, 30b. Ticktock image archive: 4tl, map page 6, 7t.

Every effort has been made to trace copyright holders, and we apologise in advance for any omissions. We would be pleased to insert the appropriate acknowledgments in any subsequent edition of this publication.

Contents

Words that look
bold like this
are in the glossary.

What is a reptile?

A reptile is an animal with a thick skin covered in **scales**. Reptiles are **ectothermic**. This means that their body **temperature** goes up or down with the temperature of the air or water around them.

This is a crocodile's foot – you can see its scaly skin.

Snakes, lizards, crocodiles, alligators, tortoises and turtles are all reptiles.

Snakes are reptiles with no legs.

Scales

Every few months, a snake wriggles out of its old skin. A shiny, new skin, a size bigger, has grown underneath.

Old skin

Lizards are reptiles. Most lizards have four legs and a tail.

If a **predator**, such as a bird, grabs a lizard's tail, the tip breaks off. The bird is left with the twitching tail. The lizard runs away and soon grows a new tail!

This agama lizard is growing a new tail – the tip is missing.

Tortoises and turtles are reptiles with shells.

A giant Galapagos tortoise

Reptile life

Adult reptiles usually live on their own. Males and females get together to **mate** and then separate again. After mating most female reptiles lay eggs, but some reptiles give birth to live babies.

This emerald tree boa gives birth to live babies.

Chameleons are tree lizards that can change their skin colour! The female shows the male she is ready to mate by changing colour.

AMAZING REPTILE FACT
Reptile eggs feel rubbery. The shell is softer than a bird's egg, but strong.

A pair of chameleons

Female

Male

Reptiles lay lots of eggs in one go. Only a few **hatch** – the rest are often eaten by other animals.

Female pythons coil their bodies around their eggs to keep them warm.

Most reptile mums leave their eggs to hatch on their own, but some reptiles look after their eggs.

When a baby reptile hatches it looks like a tiny copy of its parents. The baby is ready to find its own food right away. Baby snakes can hunt as soon as they are born.

Egg

This western pond turtle has just hatched.

What is an amphibian?

This is a toad. It looks like a frog, but has drier, bumpier skin.

An amphibian is an animal that lives in water and on land. Like reptiles, amphibians are ectothermic. Their bodies are the same temperature as the air or water around them. Amphibians have smooth skins.

Frogs, toads, newts, salamanders and caecilians are all amphibians.

This is a caecilian. It has no legs, and looks like a snake.

Newts and salamanders are amphibians with tails.

This is a fire salamander.

Most amphibians like warm, damp places with plenty of plants they can use as hiding places.

AMAZING AMPHIBIAN FACT
The word 'amphibian' means 'two lives' – one on land and one on water.

Frogs and toads are amphibians with no tails.

The bright blue colour of this poison arrow frog tells predators, "Stay away – I'm poisonous".

Amphibian life

Adult amphibians usually live on their own. Males and females get together to mate. After mating, female amphibians lay eggs. Most amphibians lay their eggs in water. This stops the eggs drying out.

Amphibian eggs have no shells. A frog's eggs look like jelly.

In the spring, male and female frogs and toads go to ponds to mate. Then the females lay eggs.

AMAZING AMPHIBIAN FACT
Male frogs puff out their throats to sing a croaky song. This attracts females.

Baby amphibians hatch from eggs. They have large heads, long tails and breathe through **gills**, like fish. Soon they grow legs and begin breathing with lungs. Then they can live on land.

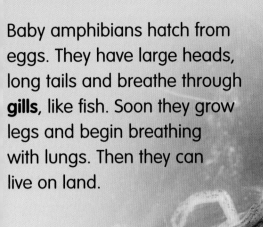

These are the young of a spotted salamander.

Most amphibians don't look after their eggs or babies, but there are some amazing amphibian parents.

Eggs

Some poison arrow frogs lay their eggs in water-filled hollows in trees. They carry the tadpoles to a new home if the water dries out.

The male midwife toad carries his eggs on his back until they hatch.

Animal habitats

A habitat is the place where a plant or an animal lives. Reptiles and amphibians live in lots of habitats from warm, wet **rainforests** to dry **grasslands**. Many amphibians live in ponds and rivers in **wetlands**.

The sea is a habitat. Turtles live in the sea.

Reptiles and amphibians live in all habitats except the Arctic and Antarctica.

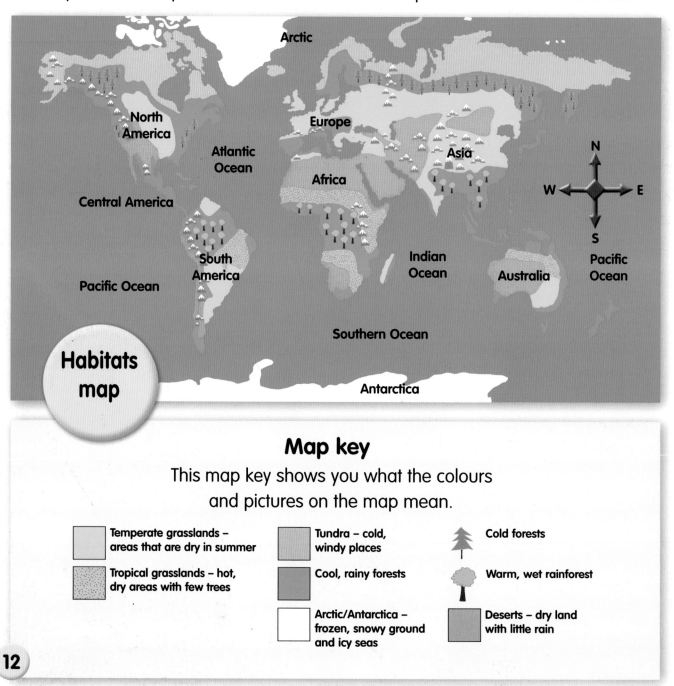

Habitats map

Arctic

North America

Europe

Asia

Atlantic Ocean

Africa

Central America

South America

Indian Ocean

Australia

Pacific Ocean

Pacific Ocean

Southern Ocean

Antarctica

N
W — E
S

Map key

This map key shows you what the colours and pictures on the map mean.

- Temperate grasslands – areas that are dry in summer
- Tropical grasslands – hot, dry areas with few trees
- Tundra – cold, windy places
- Cool, rainy forests
- Arctic/Antarctica – frozen, snowy ground and icy seas
- Cold forests
- Warm, wet rainforest
- Deserts – dry land with little rain

A marine iguana

Many snakes and lizards live in **deserts** which can be cold at night. In the morning, they lie in the sun to warm up their bodies.

This thorny devil lizard lives in deserts in Australia.

Marine iguanas live on beaches. Large, adult marine iguanas go diving in the ocean to find seaweed to eat.

Tree frogs live in forest habitats. This tree frog's green skin is good **camouflage** amongst the leaves. Its colour hides it from predators, and the insects it hunts.

AMAZING REPTILE FACT
There are over 1000 different kinds of tree frog.

13

What is a life cycle?

A life cycle is all the different **stages** and changes that a plant or animal goes through in its life. The diagrams on these pages show some examples of reptile and amphibian life cycles.

This male Jackson's chameleon uses his horns to fight other males for females.

1 A pair of rattlesnakes

A male and female snake meet and mate.

SNAKE LIFE CYCLE
All reptiles have a life cycle with these stages.

2 A female corn snake

The female lays eggs. Some snakes give birth to live babies.

4 A young emerald tree boa

Baby snakes are ready to go off on their own as soon as they hatch or are born.

3 A baby ball python

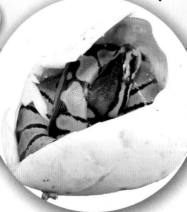

Baby snakes hatch from the eggs.

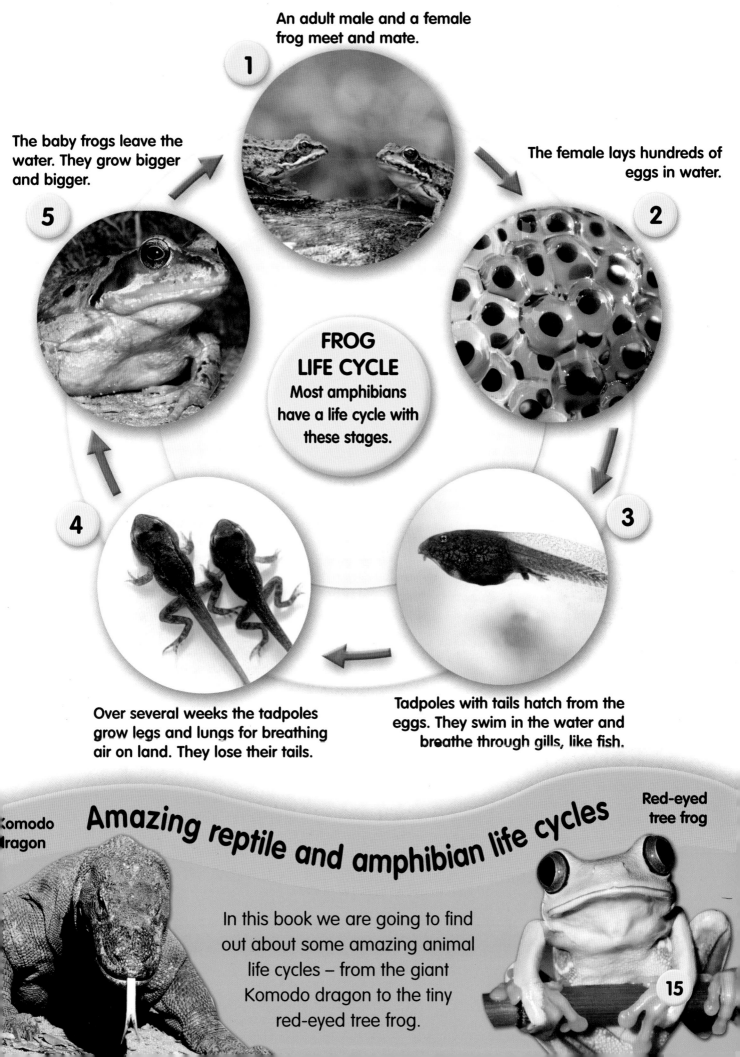

1 An adult male and a female frog meet and mate.

2 The female lays hundreds of eggs in water.

The baby frogs leave the water. They grow bigger and bigger. **5**

FROG LIFE CYCLE
Most amphibians have a life cycle with these stages.

4 Over several weeks the tadpoles grow legs and lungs for breathing air on land. They lose their tails.

3 Tadpoles with tails hatch from the eggs. They swim in the water and breathe through gills, like fish.

Amazing reptile and amphibian life cycles

Komodo dragon

Red-eyed tree frog

In this book we are going to find out about some amazing animal life cycles – from the giant Komodo dragon to the tiny red-eyed tree frog.

The egg-eating snake can
grow to one metre long.

Egg-eating snake

The egg-eating snake lives on grasslands
and in deserts in Africa. The egg-eating
snake has no teeth but it can eat a bird's
egg, bigger than its head – whole!

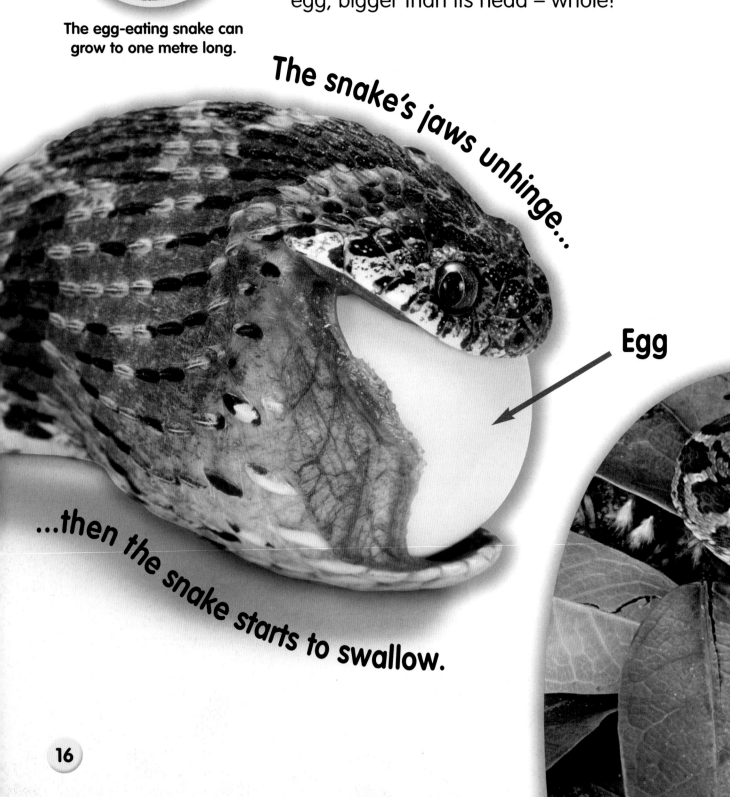

The snake's jaws unhinge...

Egg

...then the snake starts to swallow.

The snake's skin stretches around the egg.

The egg-eating snake has sharp spikes inside its throat which will crack the shell. Then the snake swallows the yolk and white, and spits out the shell.

A female egg-eating snake lays from six to 25 eggs. She scatters them around her **territory**. Then she leaves them. The eggs hatch after two to three months.

As soon as they hatch, young egg-eaters climb trees to look for eggs.

AMAZING REPTILE FACT
Before eating an egg, the snake touches it with its tongue, to make sure it is fresh.

Nile crocodile

A crocodile can bite but it cannot chew.

Nile crocodiles live beside lakes and rivers in Africa. They wait for big animals such as antelopes to come for a drink, then they grab them and eat them! Nile crocodiles also eat monkeys, turtles, birds and fish.

After she has mated, the female crocodile makes a nest beside the river. She lays between 50 and 60 eggs.

After about 60 days the eggs hatch.

Baby crocodile

AMAZING REPTILE FACT
A male Nile crocodile can grow to six metres long.

Crocodiles are fierce, but they are very good mums. They guard their eggs and even help break open the eggs with their mouths so the babies can get out.

18

The baby crocodiles call to their mum
to let her know they are hatching.

The female looks
after the babies in the
shallow water of the river.
After about eight weeks the
babies go off on their own.

The female gently carries the babies
from the nest to the river in her mouth.

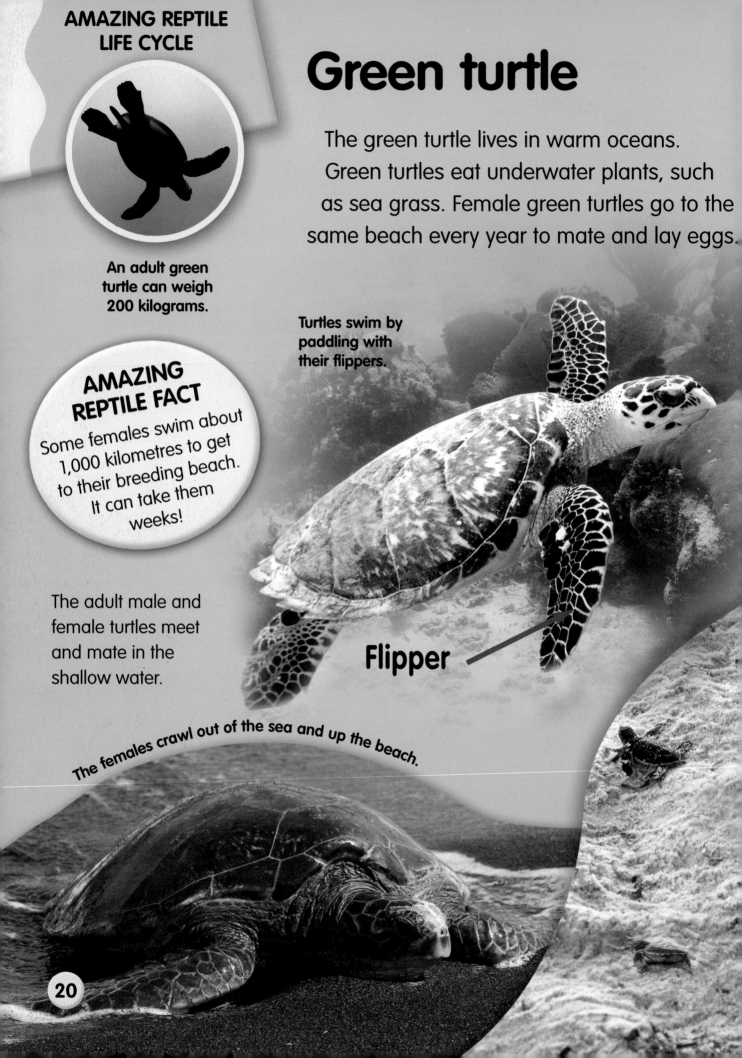

AMAZING REPTILE LIFE CYCLE

An adult green turtle can weigh 200 kilograms.

Green turtle

The green turtle lives in warm oceans. Green turtles eat underwater plants, such as sea grass. Female green turtles go to the same beach every year to mate and lay eggs.

Turtles swim by paddling with their flippers.

AMAZING REPTILE FACT

Some females swim about 1,000 kilometres to get to their breeding beach. It can take them weeks!

The adult male and female turtles meet and mate in the shallow water.

Flipper

The females crawl out of the sea and up the beach.

The green turtle lays up to 200 eggs.

The female turtle digs a deep hole in the sand with her flippers. She lays her eggs, covers them with sand, and then crawls back to the sea.

The baby turtles hatch after about seven weeks. The babies have to look after themselves. They dig out of the sand and dash to the sea.

The tiny turtle hatchlings are in danger of being eaten by predators, such as seabirds.

The dragon's spit is so full of germs, just one bite can kill its prey.

Komodo dragon

The Komodo dragon is the world's largest lizard. These giant reptiles live on Komodo Island and two other islands in South East Asia. Komodo dragons hunt for wild pigs and deer. They also eat animals that are already dead.

Male Komodos stand on their back legs to wrestle, to attract a mate.

An adult male can be three metres long!

After mating, the female scrapes out a shallow nest in the ground and lays about 25 eggs. The female then leaves the eggs to hatch on their own.

The dragon's eggs hatch after seven to nine months. The babies climb trees and eat insects and lizards. Trees are safe, because if an adult dragon catches a baby, it will eat it!

This baby dragon is two days old and about 30 centimetres long.

AMAZING REPTILE FACT
A female Komodo dragon in a British zoo laid eggs that hatched into babies even though she had no male around to mate with!

Red-eyed tree frog

The red-eyed tree frog lives in rainforests in Central America. It is a nocturnal frog. This means it rests during the day, and is active at night. Red-eyed tree frogs eat insects.

The frog's toes have suction pads to help it stick to leaves.

In the breeding season, male red-eyed tree frogs gather together on branches over a pond.

AMAZING AMPHIBIAN FACT

With its eyes closed the frog blends into its green habitat. If attacked, it opens its big red eyes – this startles predators!

The males call to females with a clicking noise.

After mating, the female lays up to 50 eggs on a leaf that's hanging over the pond. Laying lots of eggs in one go means at least some babies will survive.

After about five days the eggs hatch and the tadpoles fall down into the pond below.

Tadpole

When these tadpoles have grown into frogs, they will climb back into the trees.

Darwin's frog

The Darwin's frog lives near rivers in damp, shady, mountain forests in South America. Darwin's frogs eat insects and small animals, such as worms. The males are very good fathers.

This frog has an unusual pointy, wobbly section on the end of its nose!

When a female Darwin's frog has laid her eggs, the male guards them. After about two weeks, the babies inside the eggs start to move. Now the male picks up the eggs with his tongue and puts them into his mouth.

The eggs are in here!

The male puts up to 15 eggs into a pouch in his mouth.

The tadpoles hatch inside the male's mouth. They stay in his mouth for 50 days feeding on their egg yolks. When they have grown into little froglets, the babies climb out of dad's mouth!

AMAZING AMPHIBIAN FACT

Male frogs' pouches are normally used for croaking. When the pouches are filled with tadpoles, males can still eat, but they can't croak!

An adult Darwin's frog is just 2.5 centimetres long!

Froglet

Axolotl

If an axolotl loses a leg, it can grow another one.

The axolotl is an amphibian that looks like a baby even when it is an adult. It is a kind of salamander, but looks like a giant tadpole. Axolotls live in lakes in Mexico, in Central America, but people also keep them as pets.

The axolotl breathes through gills, not lungs, and never comes out of the water.

The axolotl is about 25 centimetres long.

Gills

Axolotls mate in water. After mating, the female lays up to 1,000 eggs and sticks them on plants and stones.

The eggs hatch in two to three weeks. The babies eat tiny water animals. Their legs start to grow after about 10 days.

Baby axolotls sometimes eat each other!

Tail

AMAZING AMPHIBIAN FACT
Some people in Mexico like to eat axolotls.

That's amazing!

Are you ready for some more amazing reptile and amphibian facts? Did you know there's a toad that doesn't have tadpoles; a snake that's as long as six men; and a lizard that's a left-over from prehistoric times

The North American bullfrog lays 25,000 eggs in one go!

These men are carrying an anaconda.

The anaconda is the world's heaviest snake. It can weigh up to 250 kilograms and grow to 10 metres long.

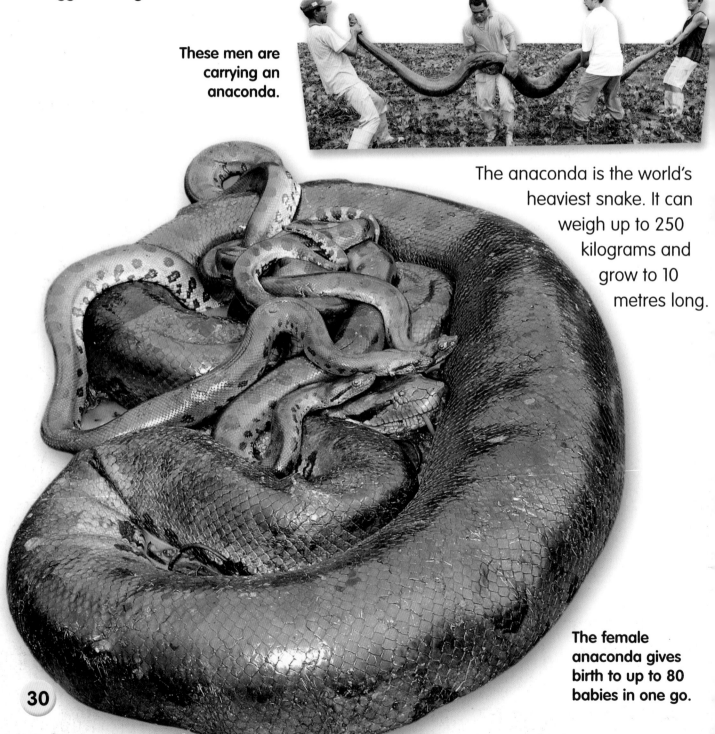

The female anaconda gives birth to up to 80 babies in one go.

There are no tadpoles in the Surinam toad's life cycle.

The female Surinam toad lays her eggs and the male puts them onto her back. A protective covering of skin grows over the eggs. When the eggs hatch, baby toads break through the skin.

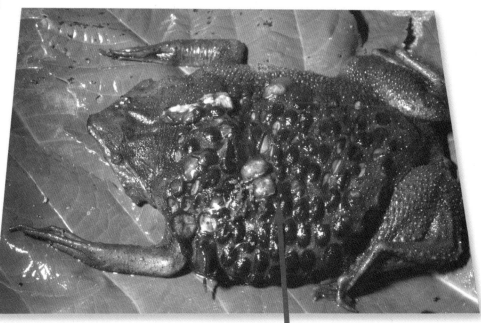

Eggs and baby toads

The tuatara is in a reptile family all of its own. Its closest relatives lived in prehistoric times, among the dinosaurs.

AMAZING REPTILE FACT
When resting, tuataras may only take one breath an hour!

Baby tuataras do not hatch from their eggs for 12 to 15 months – the longest time of any reptile.

Glossary

camouflage – Colours, marks or a shape that hides an animal from predators, and its prey.

deserts – Very dry places, that are often sandy or rocky. Deserts can be very hot in the day. Some deserts get cold at night.

ectothermic – An ectothermic animal needs sunshine to warm up and become active.

gills – Breathing organs (parts of the body) in animals that live in water, like fish and baby amphibians.

grasslands – Wide open grassy spaces with few trees.

hatch – When a baby bird or animal breaks out of its egg.

mate – When a male and female animal meet and have babies.

predator – An animal which hunts and kills other animals for food.

rainforests – Forests of tall trees in places with lots of rain.

scales – Hard plates of skin that cover the bodies of reptiles and fish.

stages – Different times in an animal's life when the animal changes.

temperature – How hot or cold something is.

territory – An area or place where an animal feeds and breeds.

wetlands – Damp places with wet, boggy ground and lots of ponds, lakes or rivers.

Index